HAL•LEONARD®
GUITAR PLAY-ALONG

AUDIO
ACCESS
INCLUDED

VOL. 20

ROCKABILLY

To access audio visit:
www.halleonard.com/mylibrary

7688-3863-8848-3083

Tracking, mixing, and mastering by Jake Johnson
All guitars by Doug Boduch
Bass by Tom McGirr
Keyboards by Warren Wiegratz
Drums by Scott Schroedl

ISBN 978-0-634-05632-1

Visit Hal Leonard Online at
www.halleonard.com

Contact us:
Hal Leonard
7777 West Bluemound Road
Milwaukee, WI 53213
Email: info@halleonard.com

In Europe, contact:
Hal Leonard Europe Limited
42 Wigmore Street
Marylebone, London, W1U 2RN
Email: info@halleonardeurope.com

In Australia, contact:
Hal Leonard Australia Pty. Ltd.
4 Lentara Court
Cheltenham, Victoria, 3192 Australia
Email: info@halleonard.com.au

ROCKABILLY

CONTENTS

Guitar Notation Legend

THE MUSICAL STAFF shows pitches and rhythms and is divided by bar lines into measures. Pitches are named after the first seven letters of the alphabet.

TABLATURE graphically represents the guitar fingerboard. Each horizontal line represents a string, and each number represents a fret.

4th string, 2nd fret   1st & 2nd strings open, played together   open D chord

HALF-STEP BEND: Strike the note and bend up 1/2 step.

WHOLE-STEP BEND: Strike the note and bend up one step.

GRACE NOTE BEND: Strike the note and bend up as indicated. The first note does not take up any time.

SLIGHT (MICROTONE) BEND: Strike the note and bend up 1/4 step.

BEND AND RELEASE: Strike the note and bend up as indicated, then release back to the original note. Only the first note is struck.

PRE-BEND: Bend the note as indicated, then strike it.

VIBRATO: The string is vibrated by rapidly bending and releasing the note with the fretting hand.

PALM MUTING: The note is partially muted by the pick hand lightly touching the string(s) just before the bridge.

HAMMER-ON: Strike the first (lower) note with one finger, then sound the higher note (on the same string) with another finger by fretting it without picking.

PULL-OFF: Place both fingers on the notes to be sounded. Strike the first note and without picking, pull the finger off to sound the second (lower) note.

LEGATO SLIDE: Strike the first note and then slide the same fret-hand finger up or down to the second note. The second note is not struck.

SHIFT SLIDE: Same as legato slide, except the second note is struck.

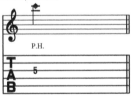

PINCH HARMONIC: The note is fretted normally and a harmonic is produced by adding the edge of the thumb or the tip of the index finger of the pick hand to the normal pick attack.

TRILL: Very rapidly alternate between the notes indicated by continuously hammering on and pulling off.

TAPPING: Hammer ("tap") the fret indicated with the pick-hand index or middle finger and pull off to the note fretted by the fret hand.

NATURAL HARMONIC: Strike the note while the fret-hand lightly touches the string directly over the fret indicated.

TREMOLO PICKING: The note is picked as rapidly and continuously as possible.

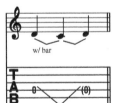

VIBRATO BAR DIVE AND RETURN: The pitch of the note or chord is dropped a specified number of steps (in rhythm) then returned to the original pitch.

VIBRATO BAR SCOOP: Depress the bar just before striking the note, then quickly release the bar.

VIBRATO BAR DIP: Strike the note and then immediately drop a specified number of steps, then release back to the original pitch.

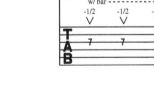

Additional Musical Definitions

   *(accent)*   • Accentuate note (play it louder)

    (staccato)   • Play the note short

D.S. al Coda   • Go back to the sign (𝄋), then play until the measure marked *"To Coda,"* then skip to the section labelled *"Coda."*

D.C. al Fine   • Go back to the beginning of the song and play until the measure marked *"Fine"* (end).

Fill   • Label used to identify a brief melodic figure which is to be inserted into the arrangement.

N.C.   • Instrument is silent (drops out).

    • Repeat measures between signs.

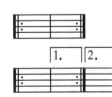   • When a repeated section has different endings, play the first ending only the first time and the second ending only the second time.

Be-Bop-A-Lula

Words and Music by Tex Davis and Gene Vincent

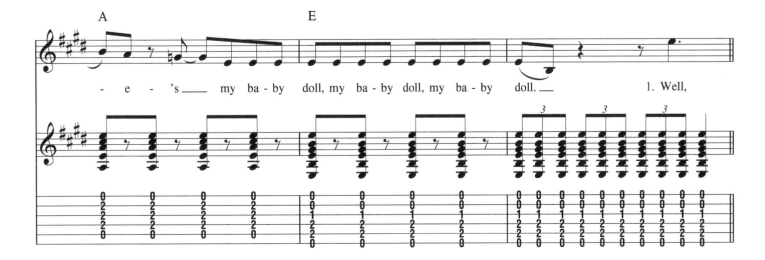

-e-'s __ my ba-by doll, my ba-by doll, my ba-by doll. __ 1. Well,

Verse

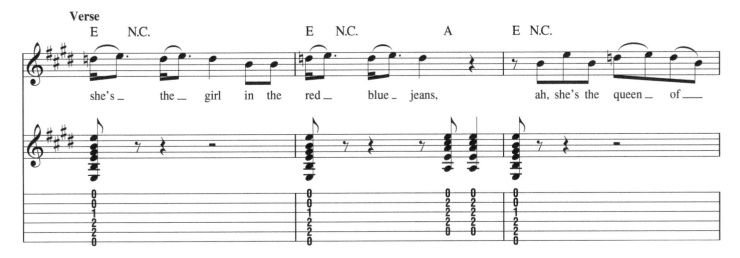

she's __ the __ girl in the red __ blue __ jeans, ah, she's the queen __ of __

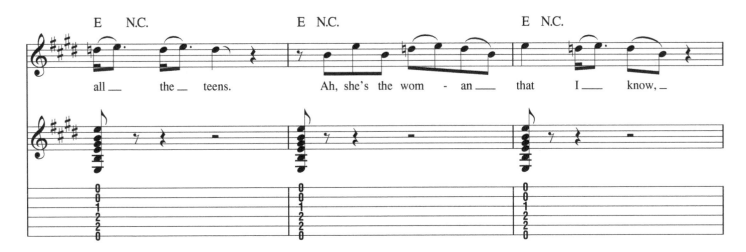

all __ the __ teens. Ah, she's the wom-an __ that I __ know, __

Chorus

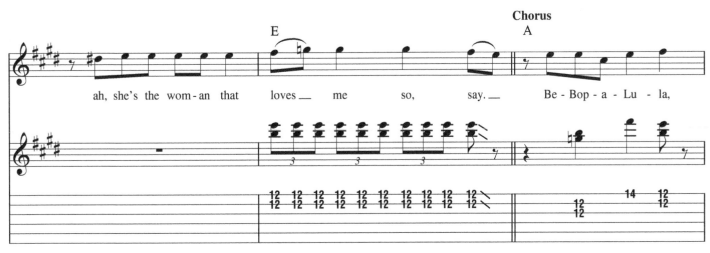

ah, she's the wom-an that loves __ me so, say. __ Be-Bop-a-Lu-la,

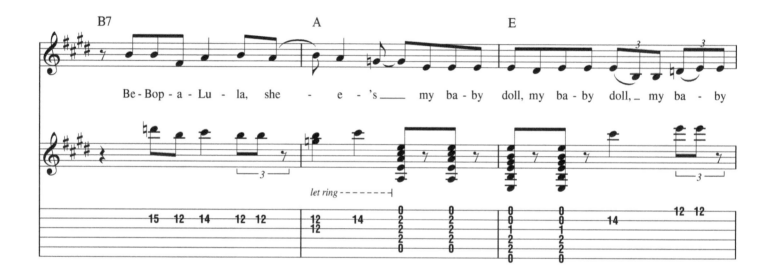

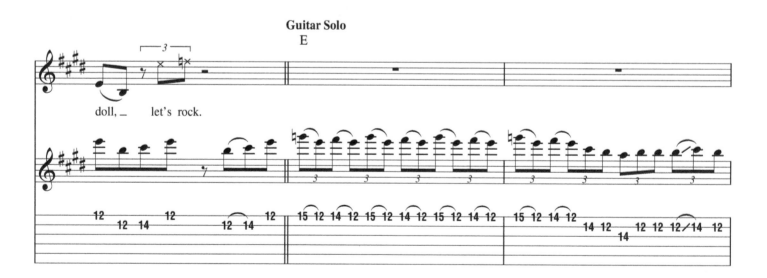

Guitar Solo

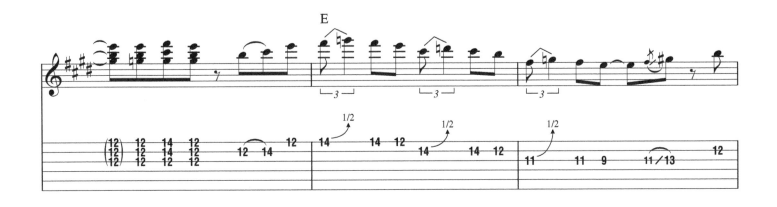

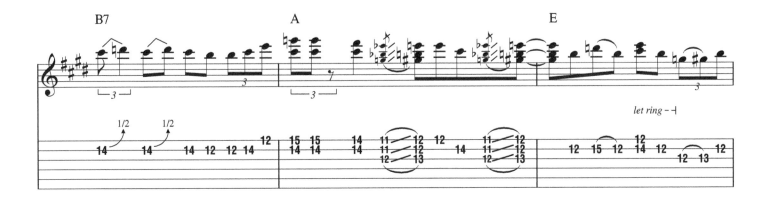

2.Well, ___ now she's ___ the wom-an that's got that beat,

oh, she's the wom-an with the fly - in' ___ feet. Ah, she's the wom-an that walks a -

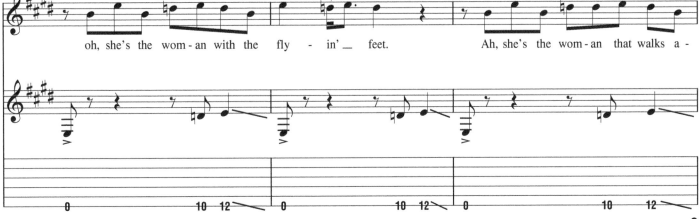

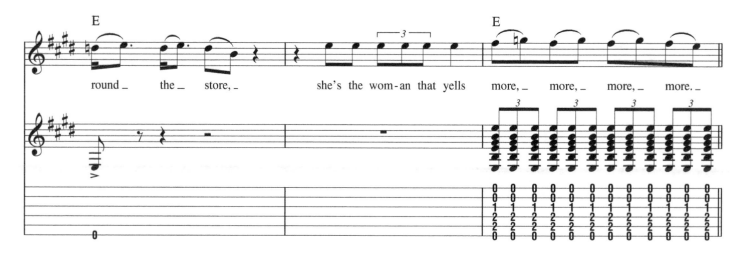

round __ the __ store, __ she's the wom-an that yells more, __ more, __ more, __ more. __

Chorus

w/ pick & fingers

Be - Bop - a - Lu - la, she's my ___ ba - by. Be - Bop - a - Lu - la, I

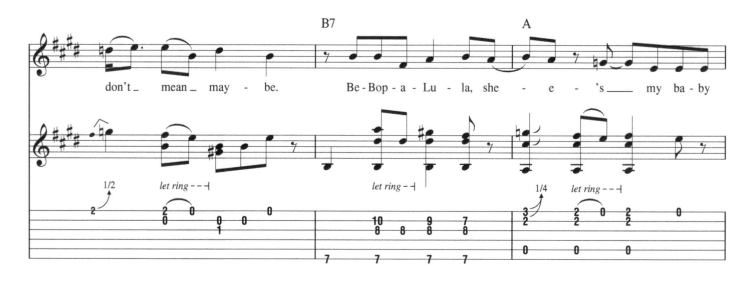

don't __ mean __ may - be. Be - Bop - a - Lu - la, she - e - 's ___ my ba - by

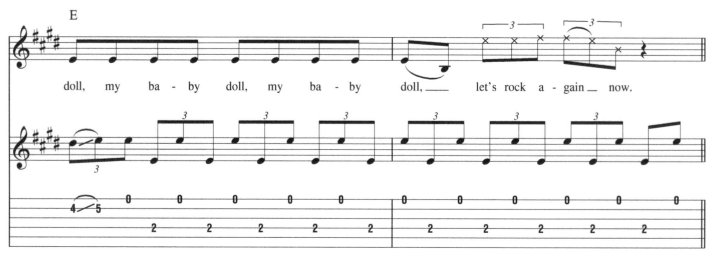

doll, my ba - by doll, my ba - by doll, ___ let's rock a - gain __ now.

Guitar Solo

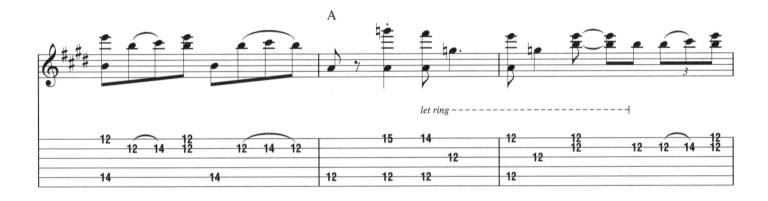

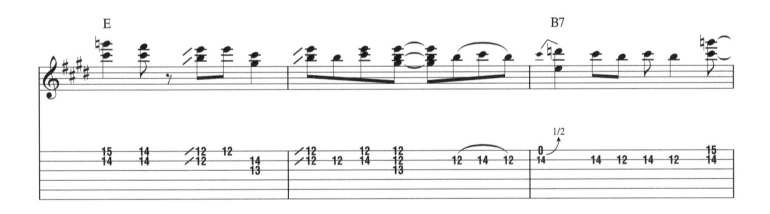

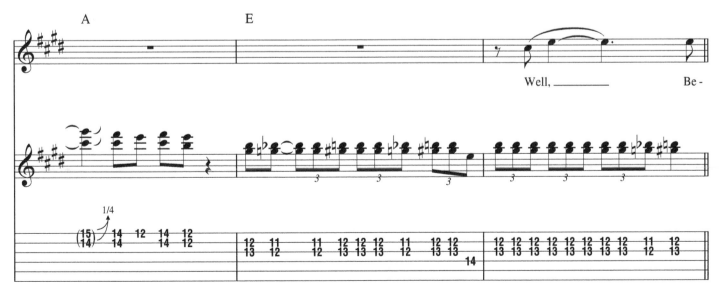

Well, _____ Be-

Chorus

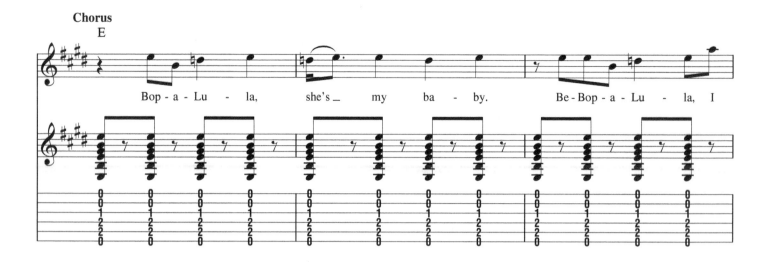

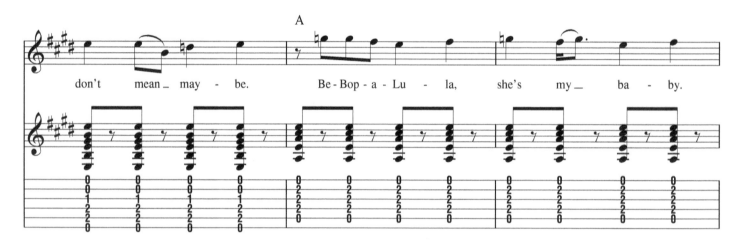

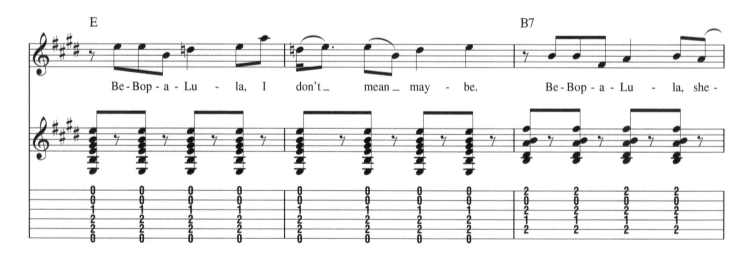

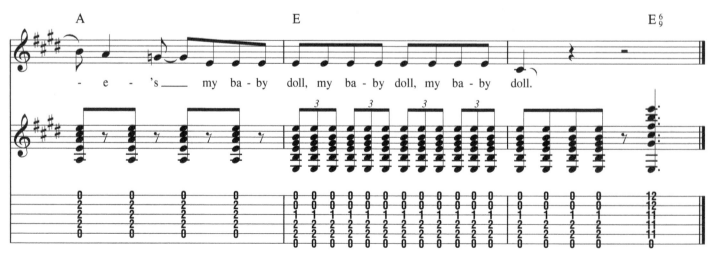

Hello Mary Lou

Words and Music by Gene Pitney and C. Mangiaracina

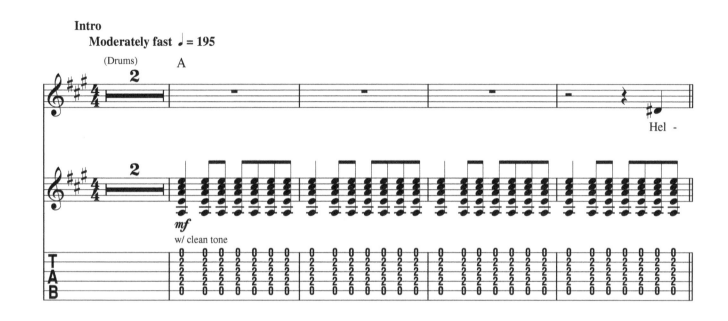

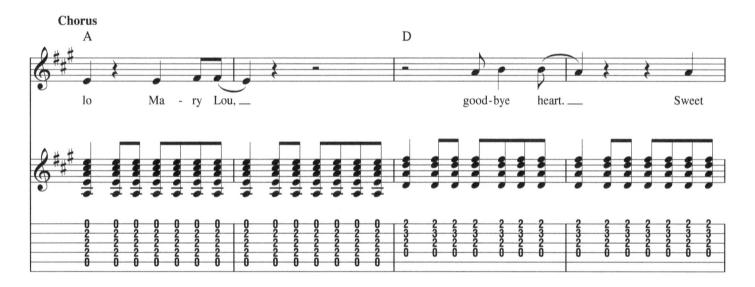

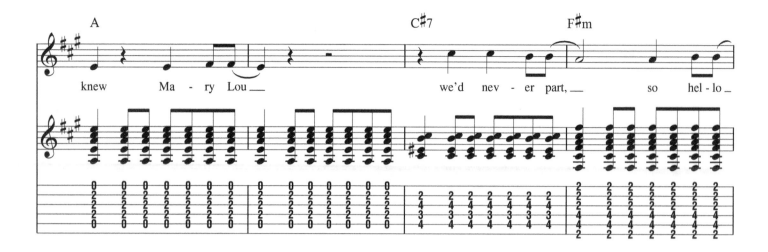

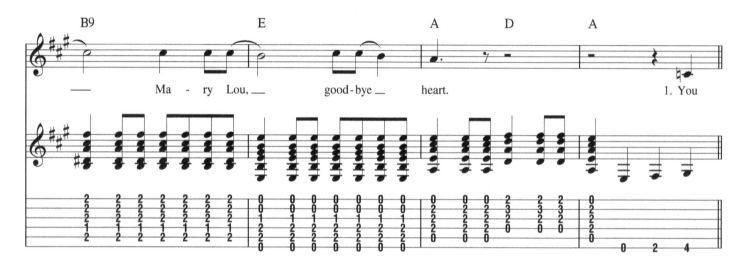

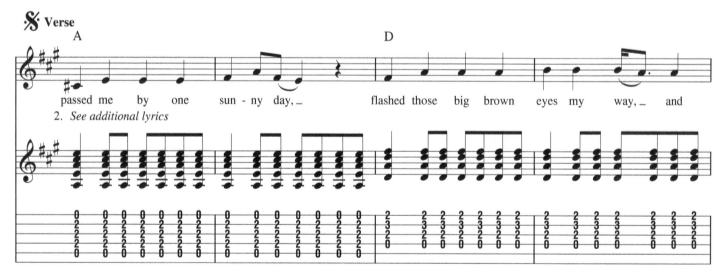

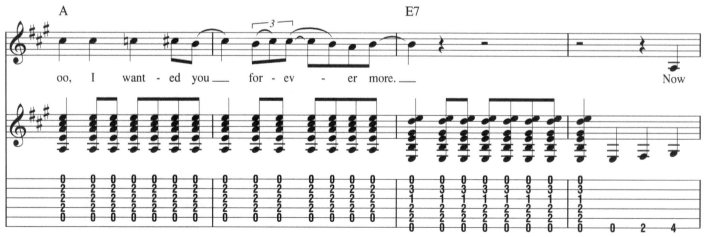

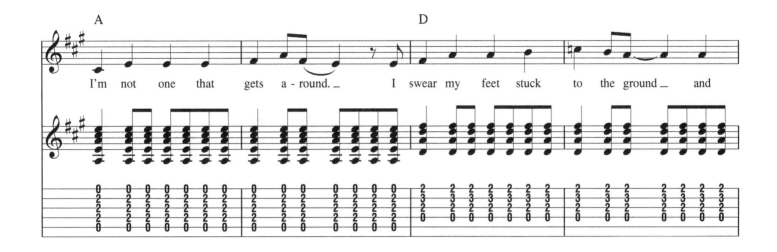

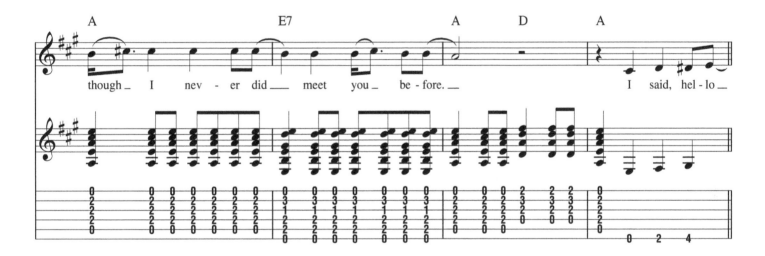

Chorus

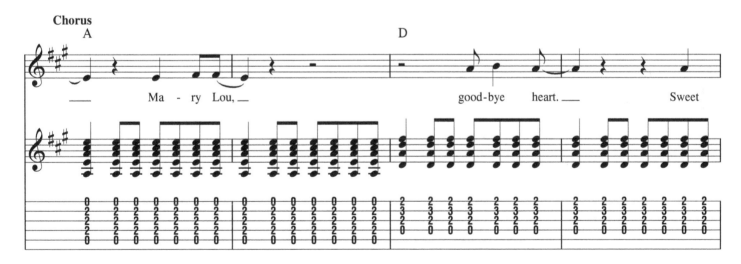

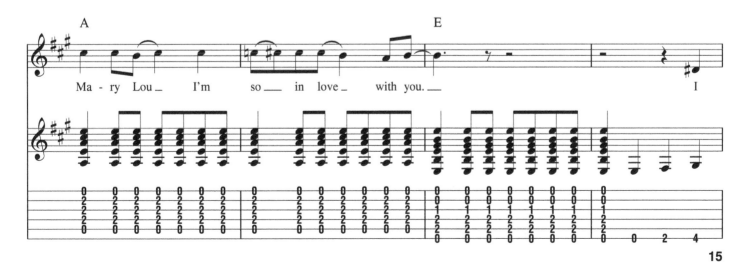

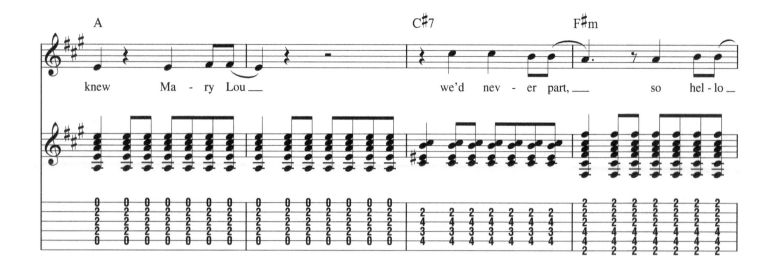

knew Ma - ry Lou ___ we'd nev - er part, ___ so hel - lo ___

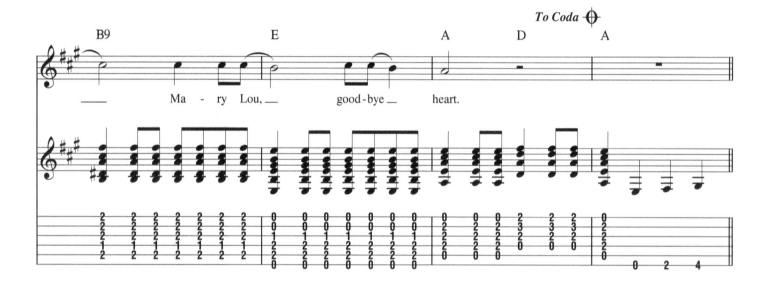

Ma - ry Lou, ___ good - bye ___ heart.

Guitar Solo

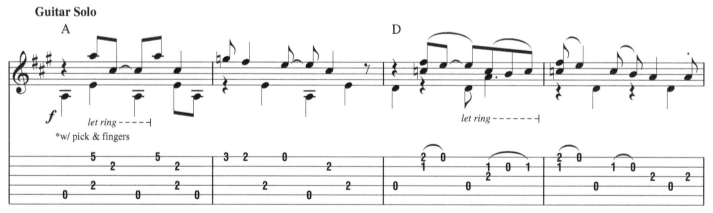

*w/ pick & fingers

*P.M. downstemmed notes throughout.

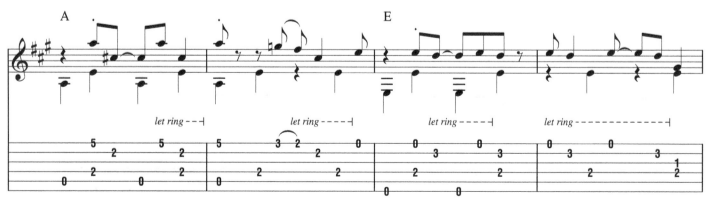

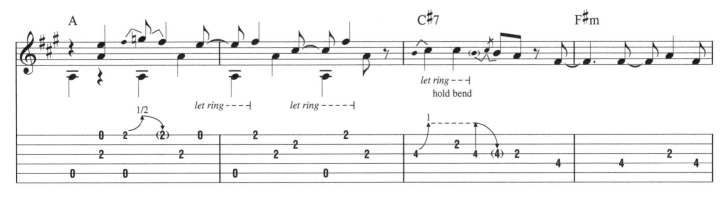

D.S. al Coda

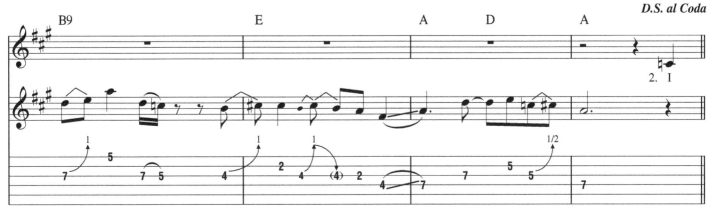

$\bigoplus$ **Coda**

Outro

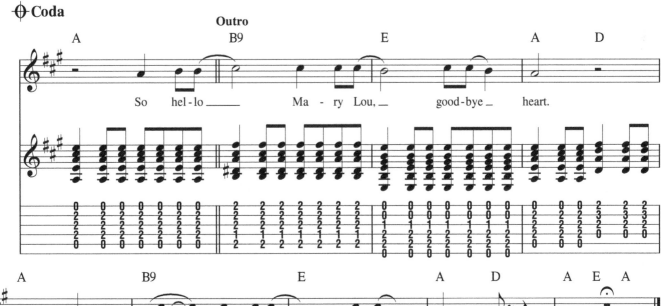

So hel - lo _____ Ma - ry Lou, _____ good-bye _____ heart.

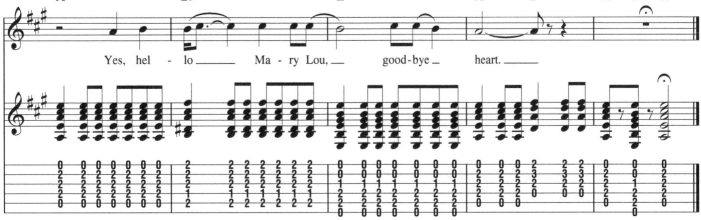

Yes, hel - lo _____ Ma - ry Lou, _____ good-bye _____ heart. _____

Additional Lyrics

2. I saw your lips, I heard your voice,
   Believe me I just had no choice.
   Wild horses couldn't make me stay away.
   I thought about a moonlit night,
   My arms around you good an' tight.
   That's all I had to see for me to say.

Blue Suede Shoes

Words and Music by Carl Lee Perkins

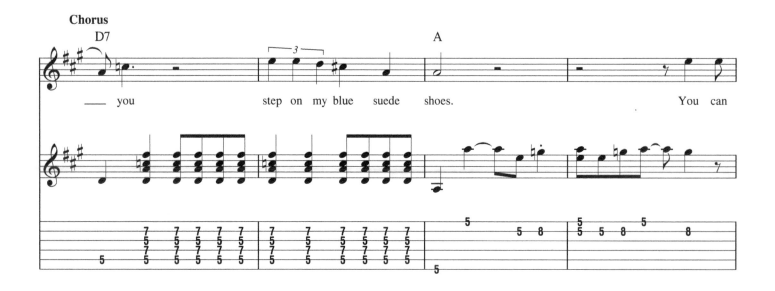

you   step on my blue suede shoes.   You can

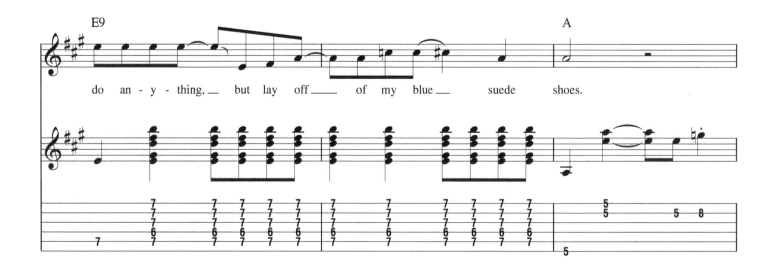

do an-y-thing, __ but lay off __ of my blue __ suede shoes.

To Coda 1

Guitar Solo

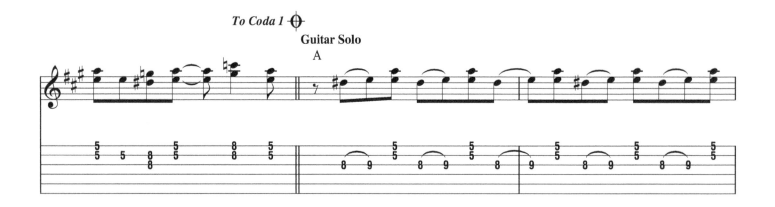

D.S. al Coda 1

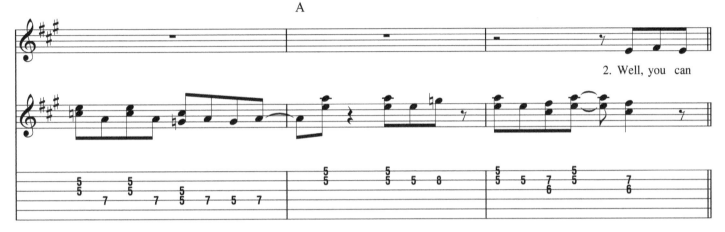

2. Well, you can

⊕ Coda 1
Guitar Solo

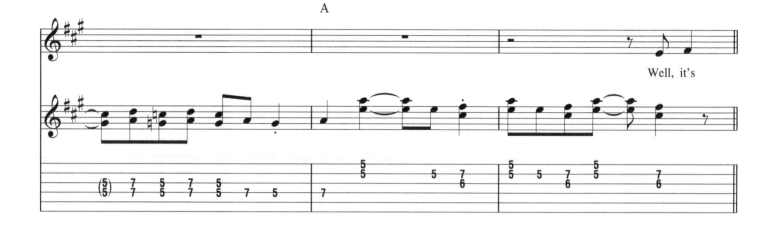

A

Well, it's

Chorus

D.S.S. al Coda 2

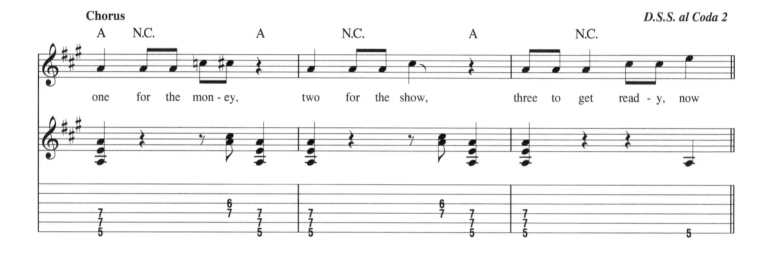

A   N.C.   A   N.C.   A   N.C.

one   for the mon - ey,   two   for the show,   three   to get read - y, now

⊕ Coda 2

Outro-Chorus

A

Well, it's   blue,   blue,   blue suede   shoes,

D7

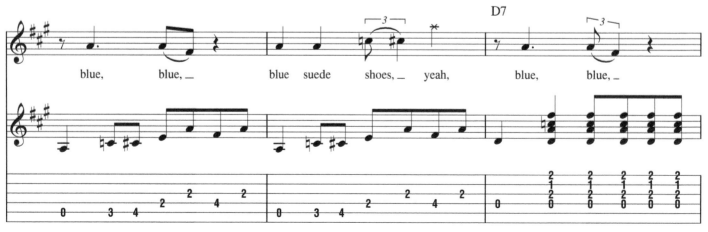

blue,   blue, __   blue suede   shoes, __ yeah,   blue,   blue, __

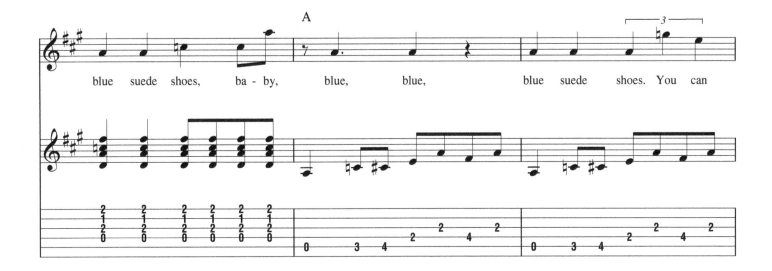

blue suede shoes, ba - by, blue, blue, blue suede shoes. You can

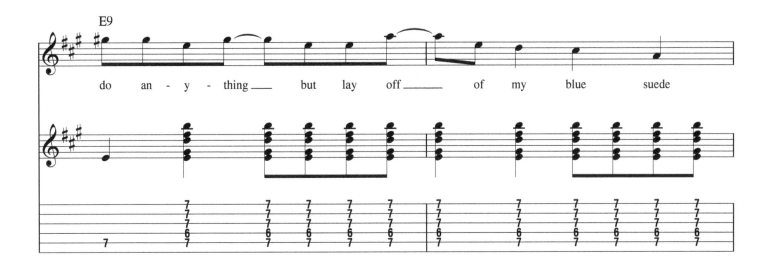

do an - y - thing ____ but lay off ____ of my blue suede

shoes.

Additional Lyrics

2. Well, you can burn my house, steal my car,
   Drink my liquor from an old fruit jar,
   And do anything that you wanna do,
   But uh-uh, honey, lay off of them shoes,
   And don't you ...

Little Sister

Words and Music by Doc Pomus and Mort Shuman

Intro

Moderate Rock ♩ = 138

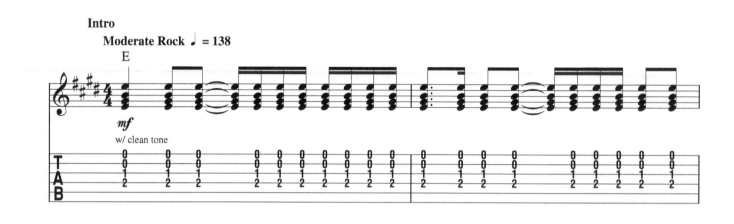

mf

w/ clean tone

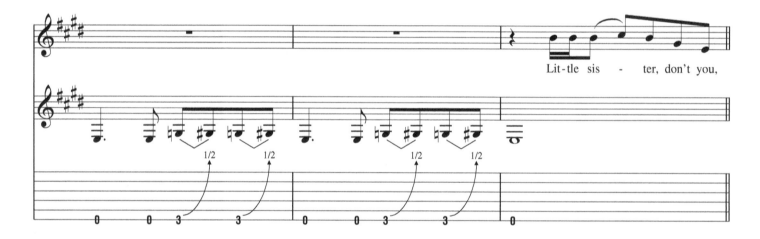

Lit-tle sis - ter, don't you,

𝄋 **Chorus**

2nd & 3rd times, substitute Fill 1

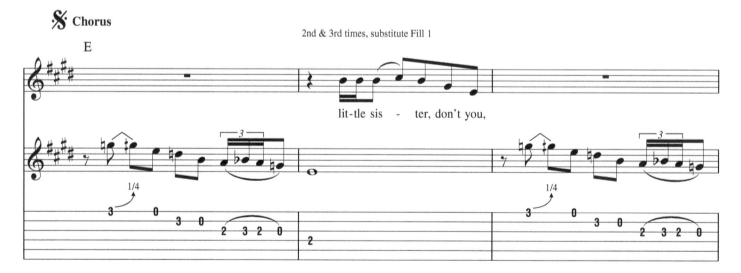

lit-tle sis - ter, don't you,

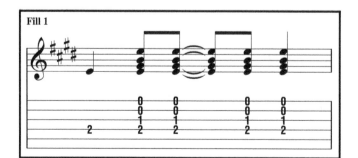

Fill 1

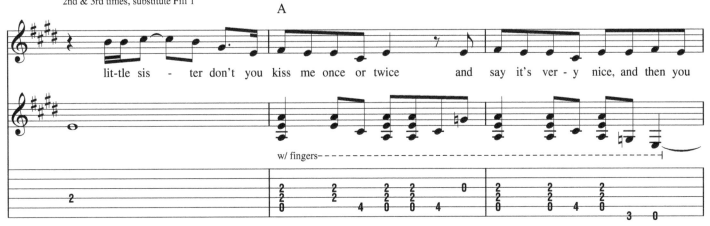

lit-tle sis - ter don't you kiss me once or twice and say it's ver - y nice, and then you

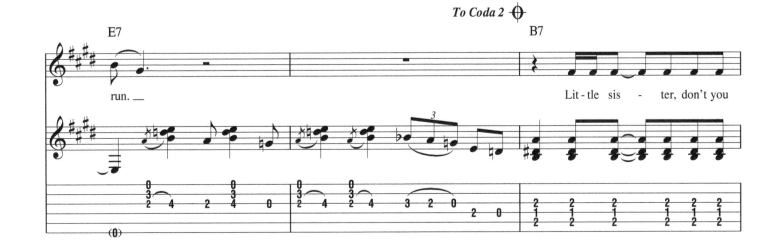

run. ___ Lit - tle sis - ter, don't you

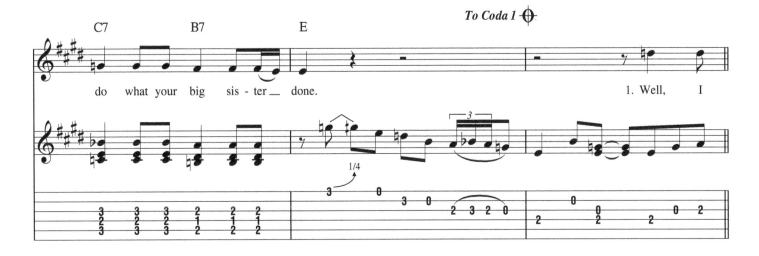

do what your big sis - ter __ done. 1. Well, I

Verse

dat - ed your big sis - ter, and I took her __ to a show. __

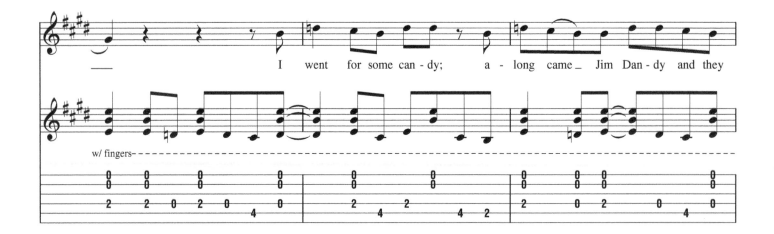

I went for some can-dy; a - long came Jim Dan - dy and they

w/ fingers------

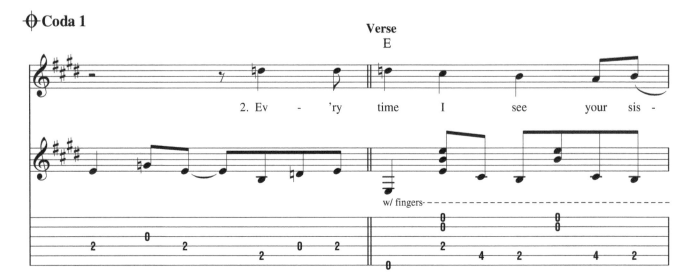

D.S. al Coda 1

N.C.   E   N.C.

snuck right out the door.   Lit - tle sis - ter, don't you,

w/ fingers--

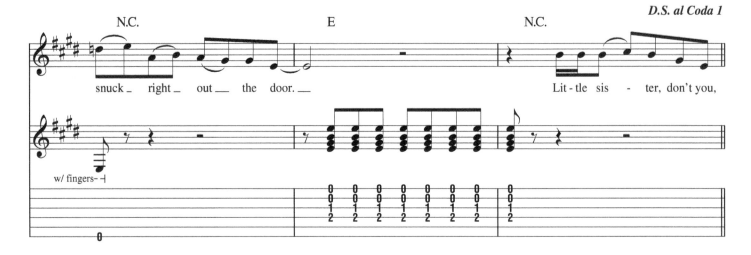

Coda 1

Verse
E

2. Ev - 'ry time I see your sis -

w/ fingers-------------

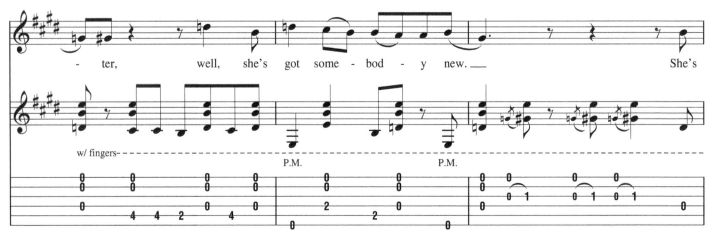

- ter, well, she's got some - bod - y new.   She's

w/ fingers-------------   P.M.   P.M.

mean and she's e - vil, like that lit - tle old ___ boll wee - vil; guess I'll

w/ fingers- -
P.M.   P.M.

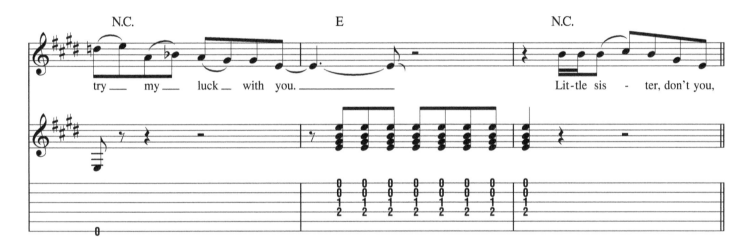

N.C.   E   N.C.

try ___ my ___ luck ___ with you. _____ Lit-tle sis - ter, don't you,

Chorus
E

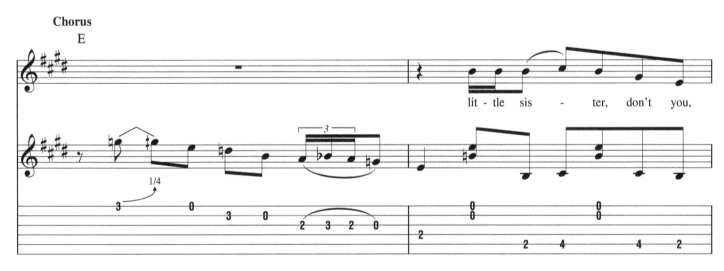

lit - tle sis - ter, don't you,

A

lit - tle sis - ter, don't you, kiss me once or twice and

w/ fingers- -

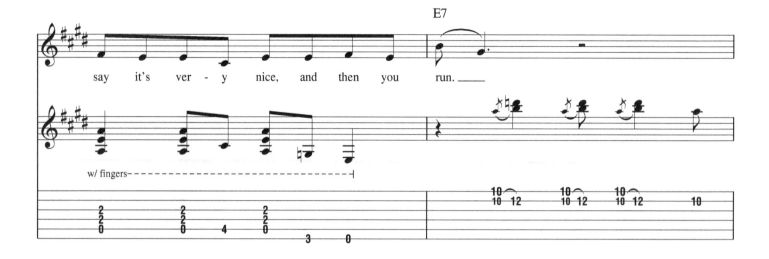

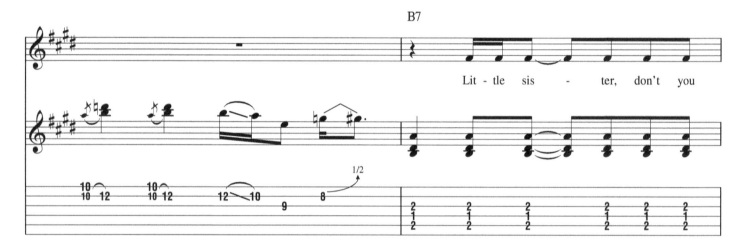

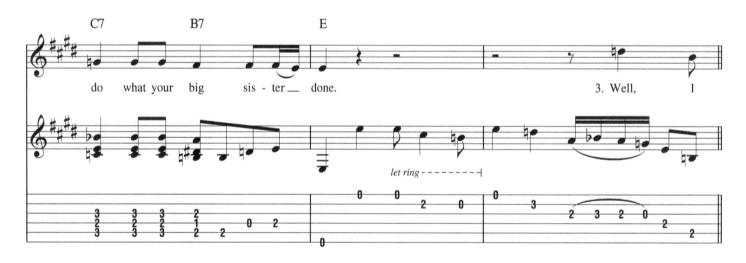

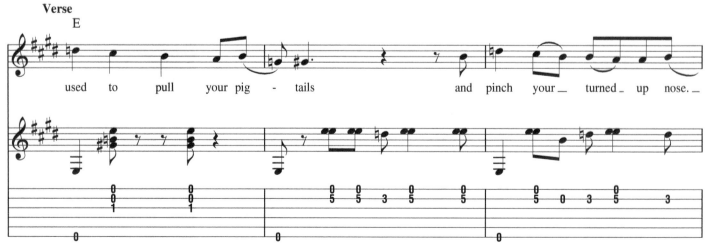

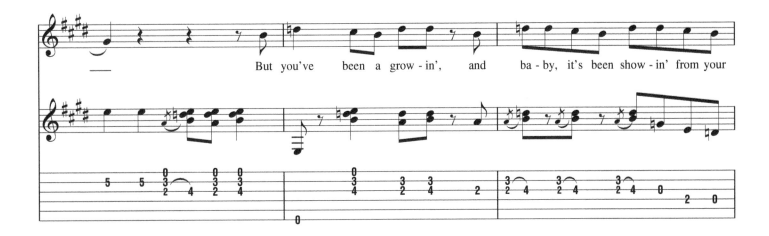

But you've been a grow - in', and ba - by, it's been show - in' from your

D.S. al Coda 2

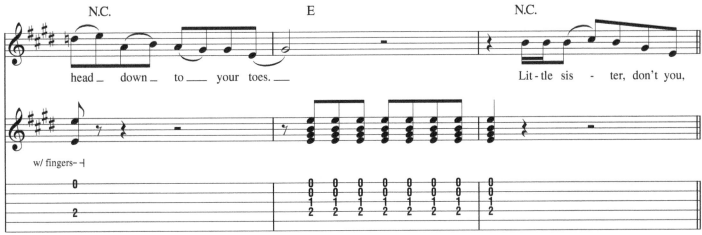

N.C.   E   N.C.

head _ down _ to _ your toes. _   Lit - tle sis - ter, don't you,

w/ fingers

⊕ Coda 2

Outro

B7   C7   B7

Lit - tle sis - ter, don't you   do   what your   big   sis - ter _

Repeat and fade

E

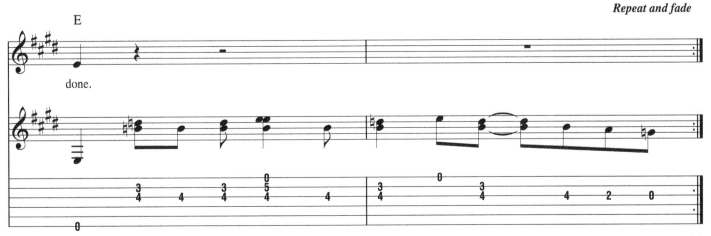

done.

Rock This Town

Words and Music by Brian Setzer

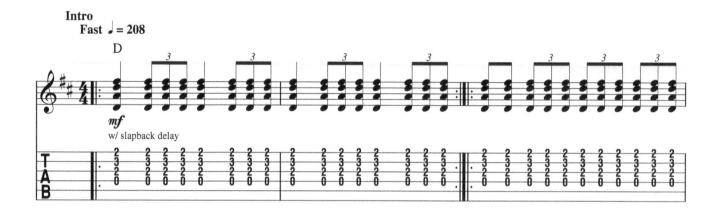

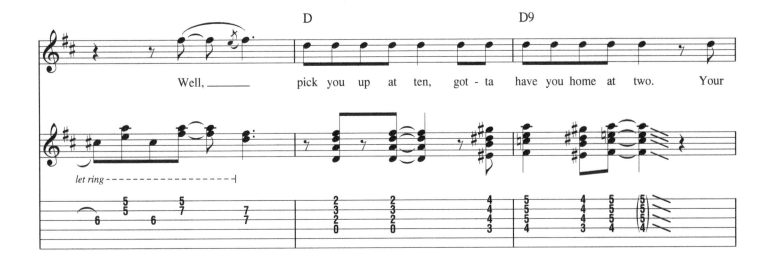

Well, _____ pick you up at ten, got-ta have you home at two. Your

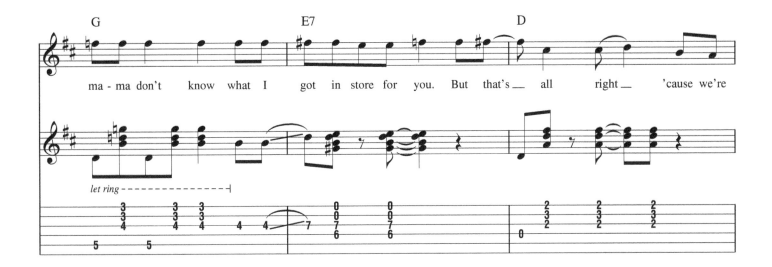

ma - ma don't know what I got in store for you. But that's ___ all right ___ 'cause we're

Interlude

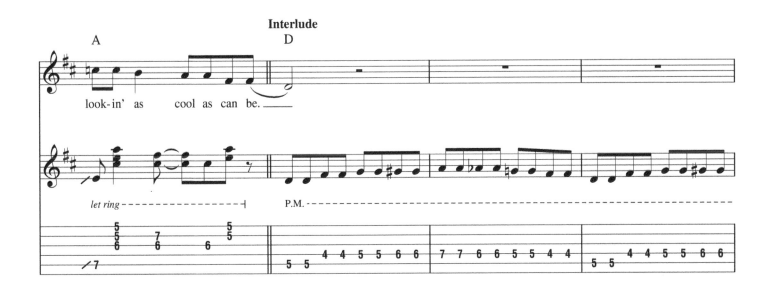

look-in' as cool as can be. ___

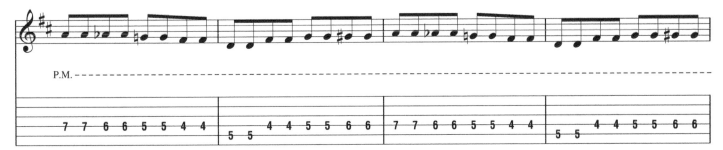

Verse

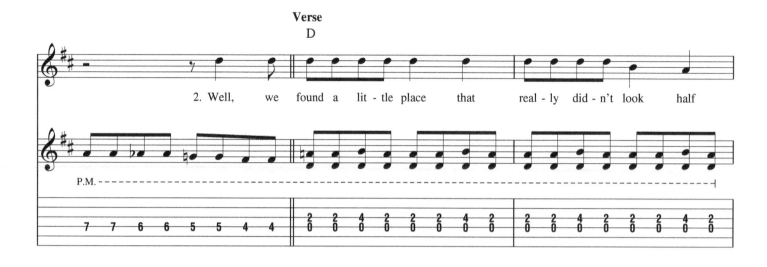

2. Well, we found a lit-tle place that real-ly did-n't look half

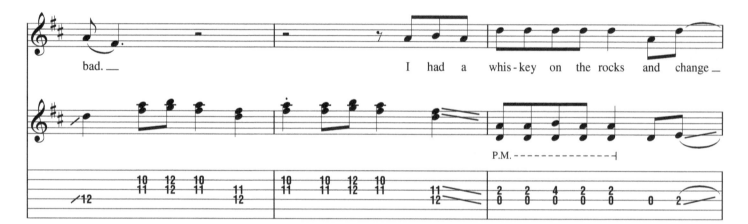

bad. ___ I had a whis-key on the rocks and change ___

___ of a dol-lar for the juke - box. Well, ___ I

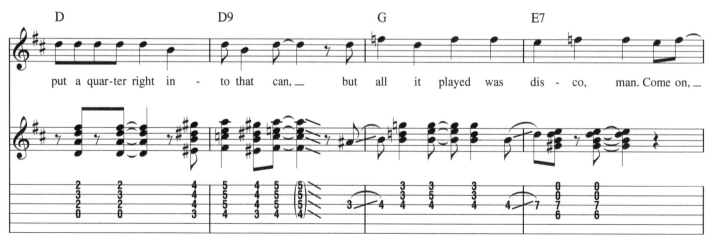

put a quar-ter right in - to that can, ___ but all it played was dis - co, man. Come on, ___

pret - ty ba - by, let's get out of here right a - way. ___ We're gon-na

𝄋 Chorus

2nd time, substitute Fill 1

rock this town, rock __ it in - side out. ___ We're gon-na

P.M. ----------------------------------

3rd time, substitute Fill 2

rock this town, make __ 'em scream __ and shout. _____

P.M. ---

Fill 1

P.M. ---

Fill 2

P.M. ---------------------- *let ring* ----------- *let ring* -----------

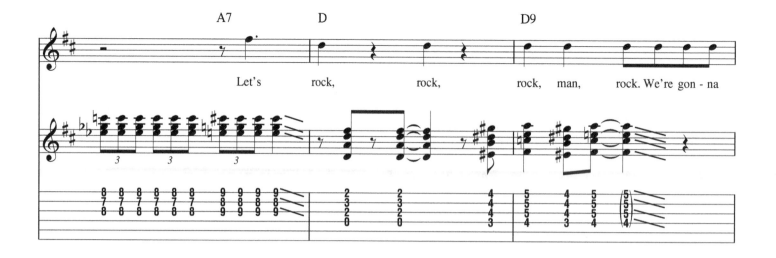

Let's rock, rock, rock, man, rock. We're gon - na

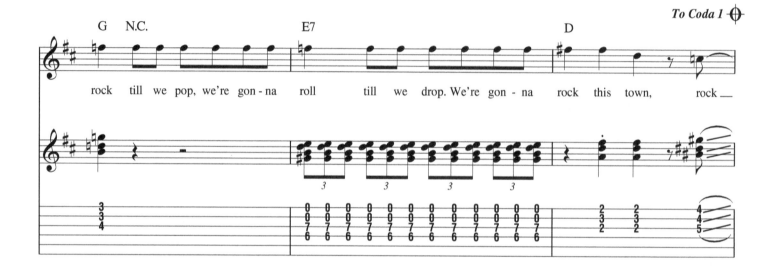

rock till we pop, we're gon - na roll till we drop. We're gon - na rock this town, rock ___

To Coda 1

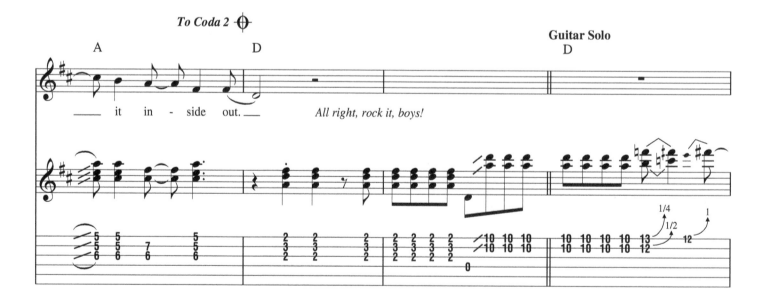

To Coda 2

___ *it in - side out.* ___ *All right, rock it, boys!*

Guitar Solo

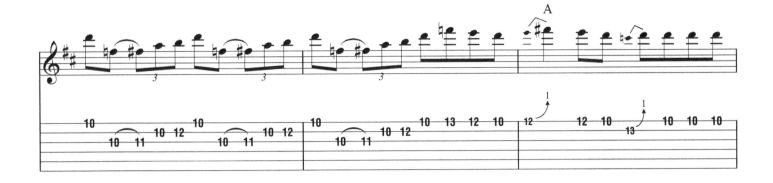

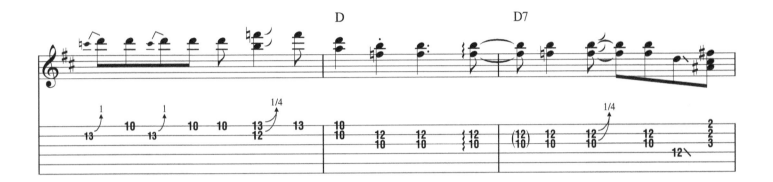

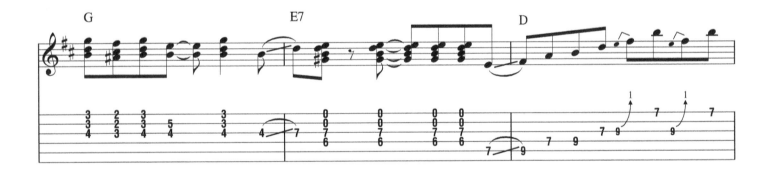

Interlude

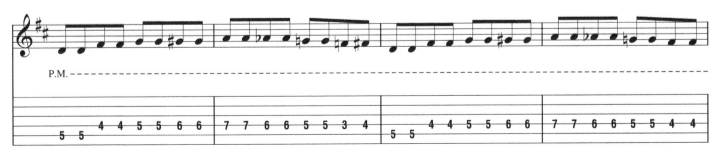

3. Well, we're hav - in' a ball ___ just a

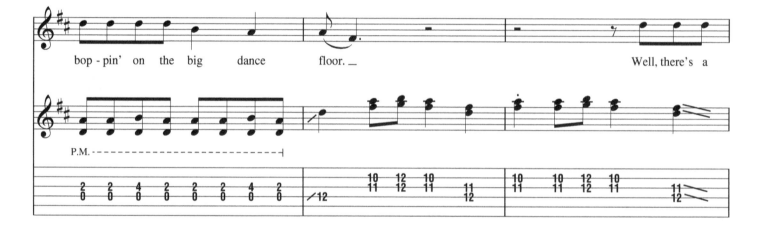

bop - pin' on the big dance floor. ___ Well, there's a

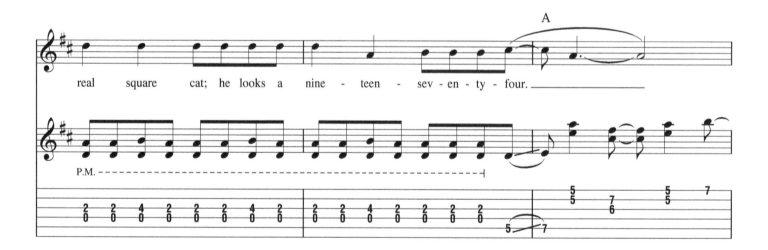

real square cat; he looks a nine - teen - sev - en - ty - four. _____

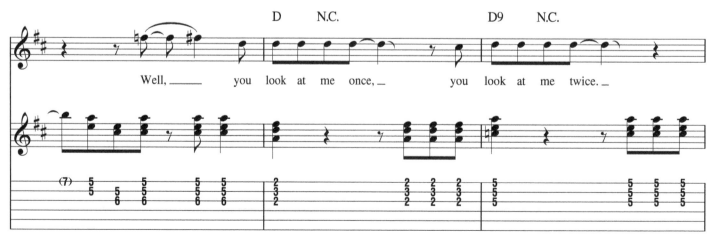

Well, ___ you look at me once, ___ you look at me twice. ___

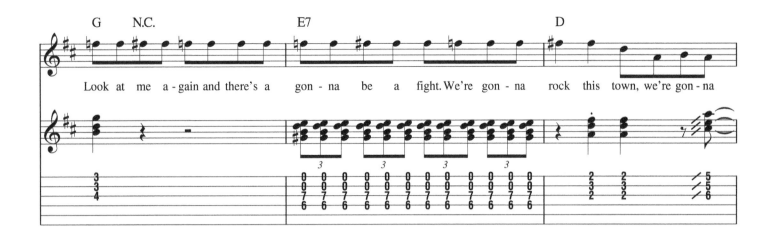

Look at me a - gain and there's a gon - na be a fight. We're gon - na rock this town, we're gon - na

D.S. al Coda 1

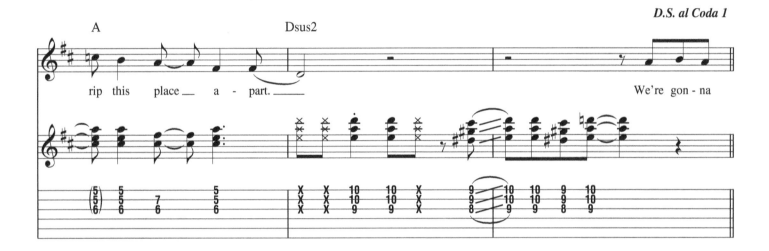

rip this place __ a - part. __ We're gon - na

⊕ Coda 1

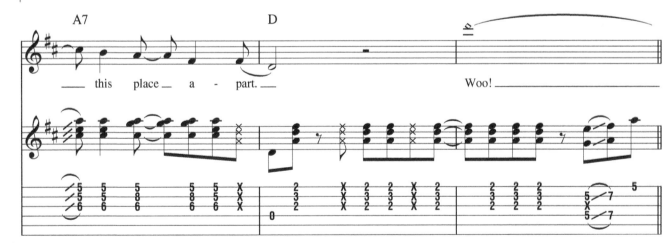

__ this place __ a - part. __ Woo! __

Guitar Solo

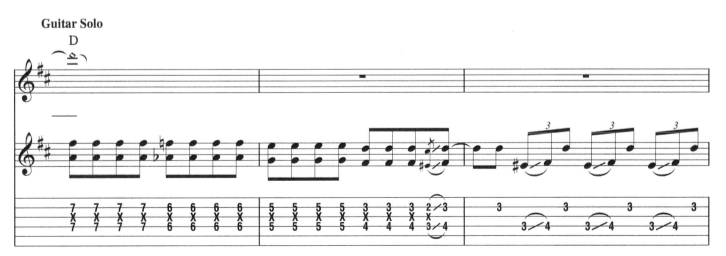

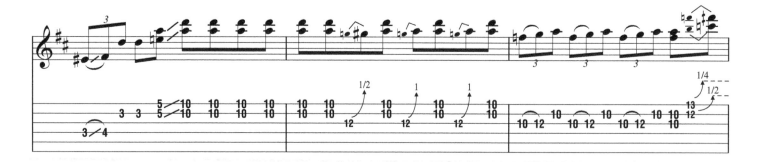

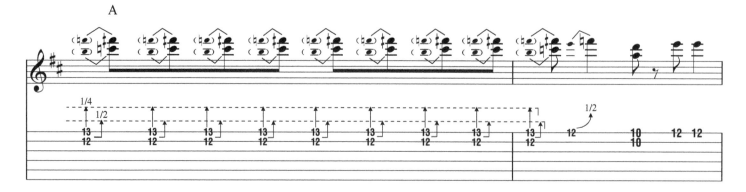

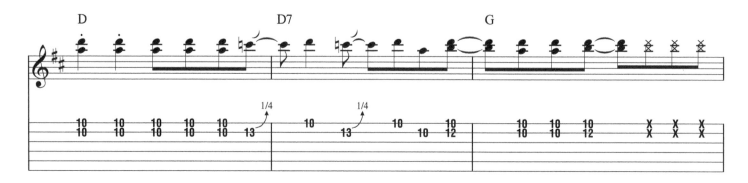

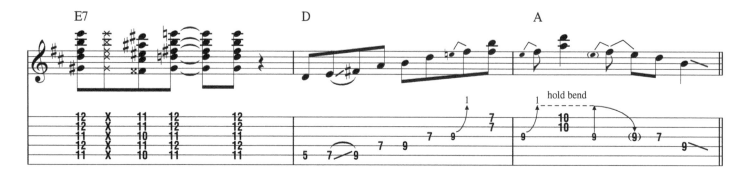

1., 2., 3.

4.

D.S. al Coda 2

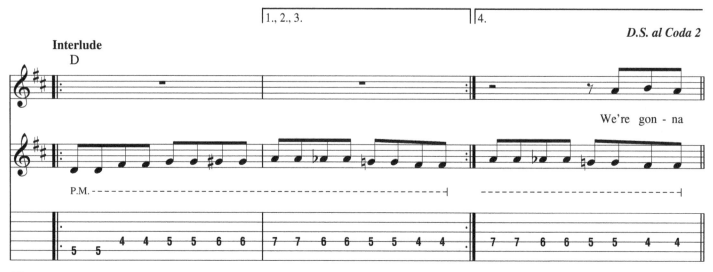

Interlude

We're gon - na

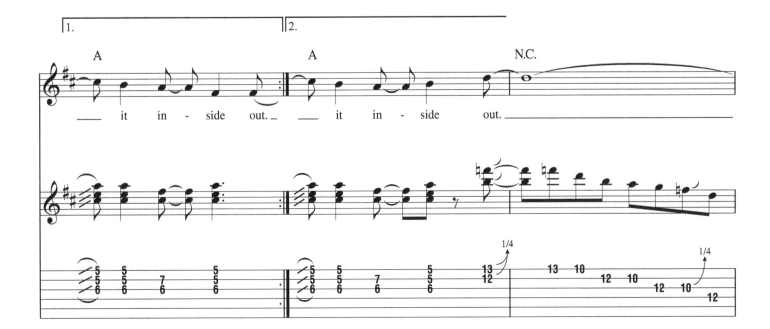

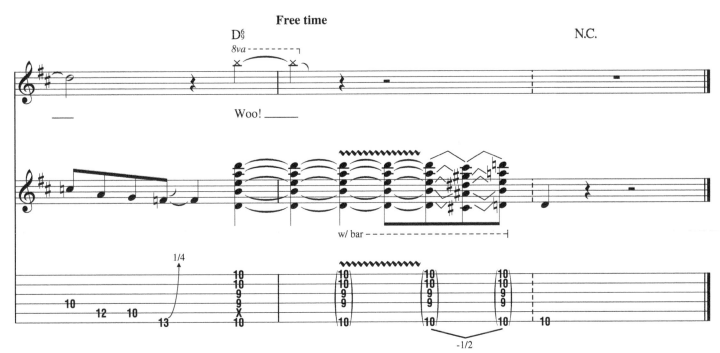

Stray Cat Strut

Words and Music by Brian Setzer

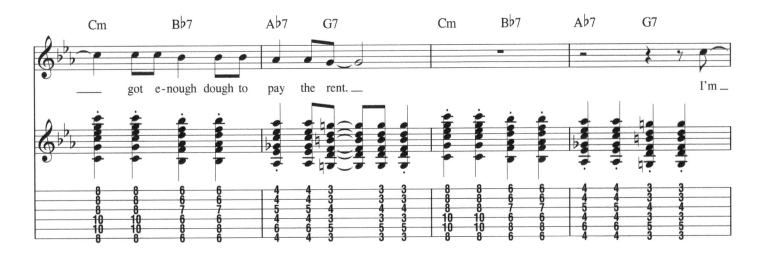

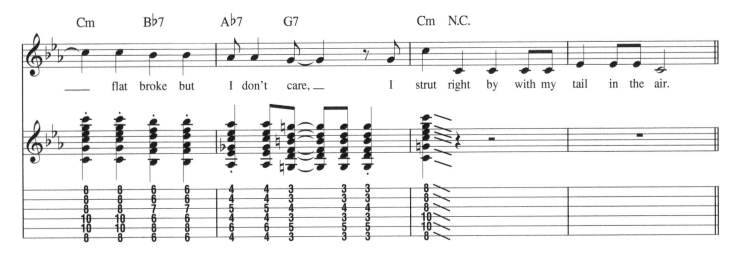

Chorus

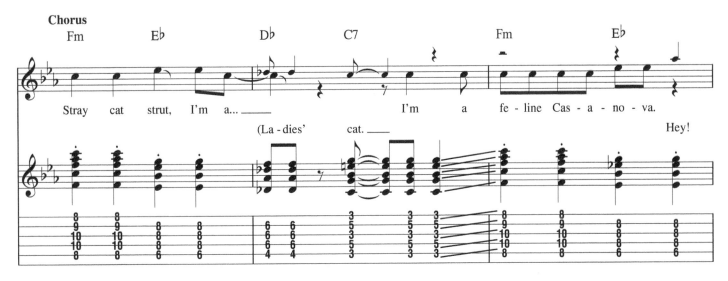

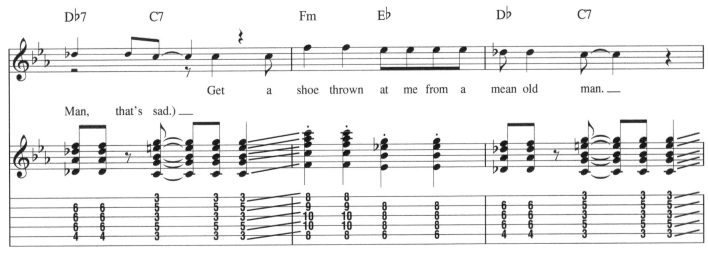

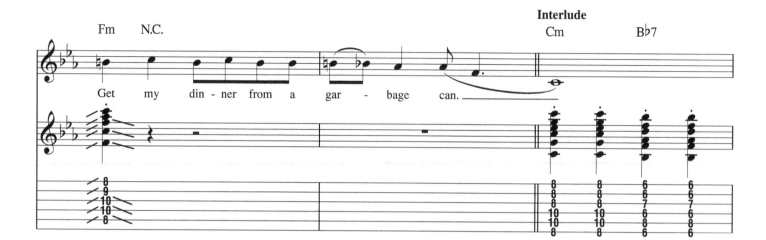

Get my din - ner from a gar - bage can. _____

Interlude

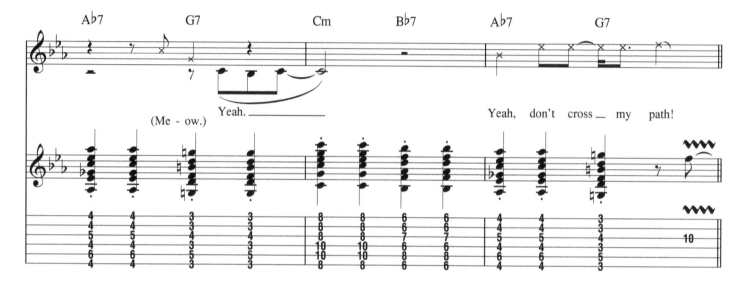

(Me - ow.)   Yeah. _____   Yeah, don't cross _____ my path!

Guitar Solo

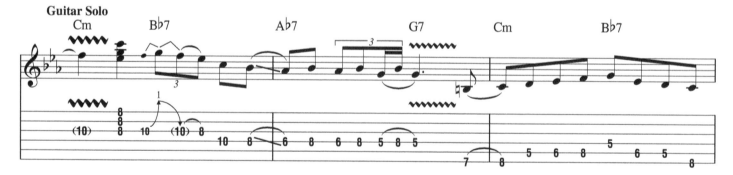

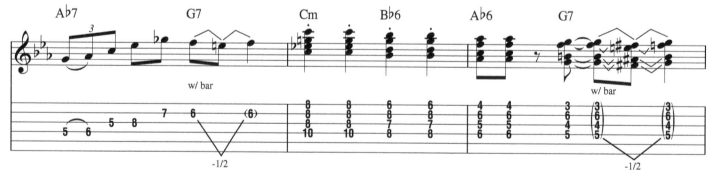

w/ bar   w/ bar

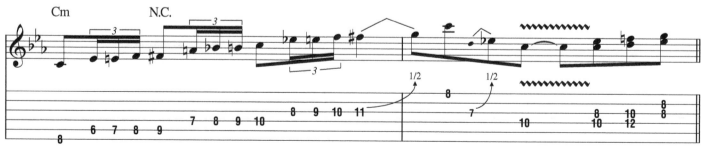

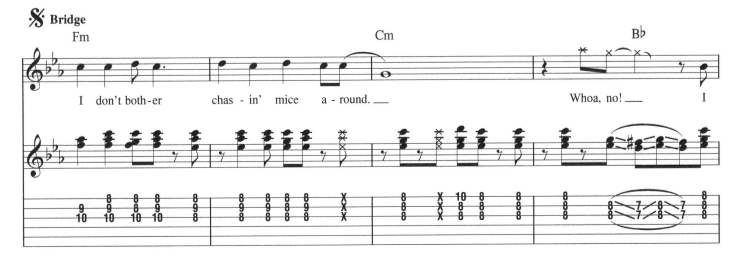

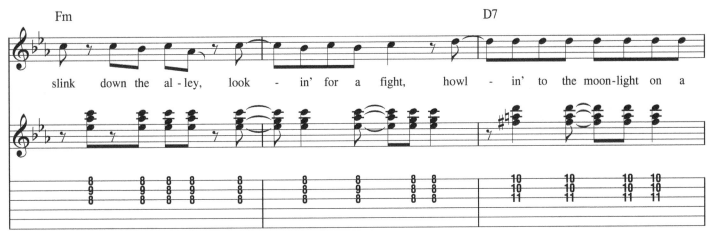

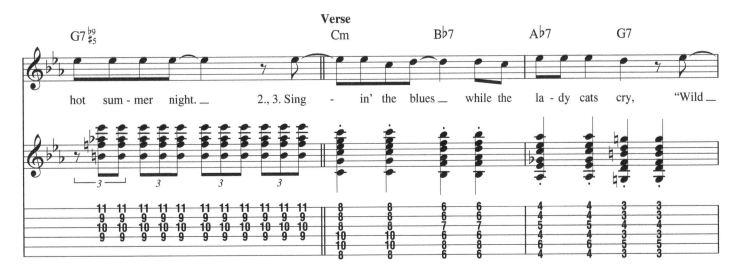

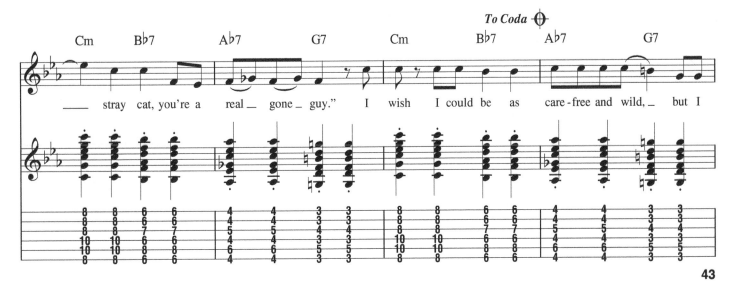

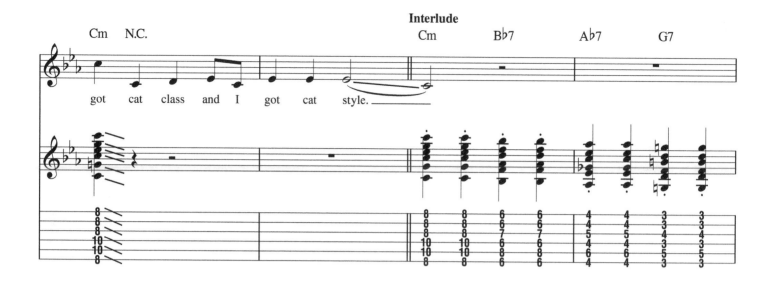

got cat class and I got cat style. ____

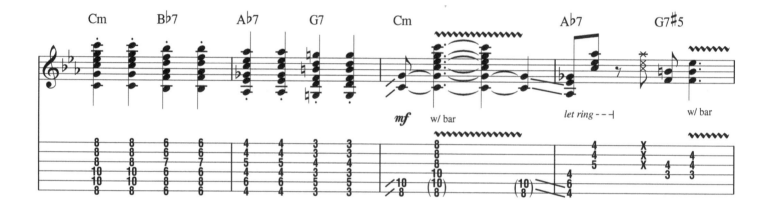

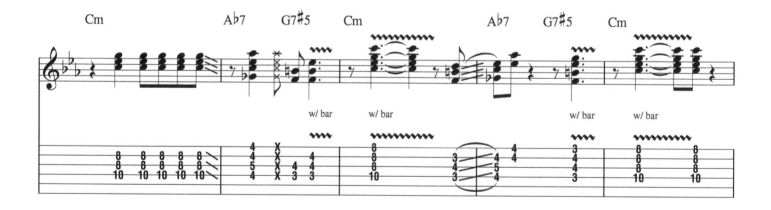

Guitar Solo

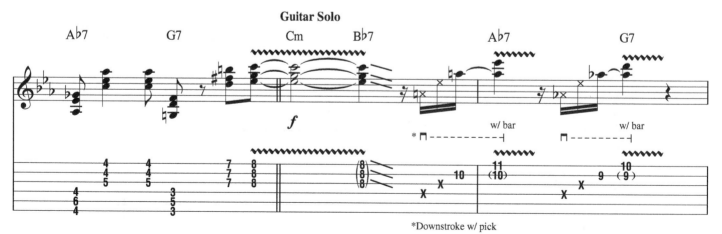

*Downstroke w/ pick

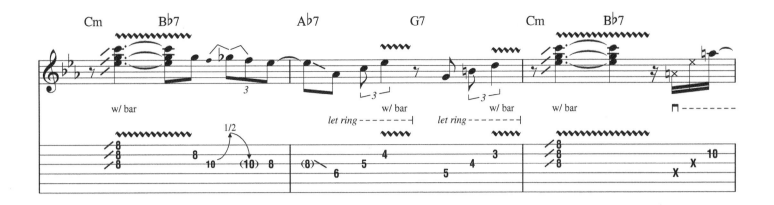

D.S. al Coda

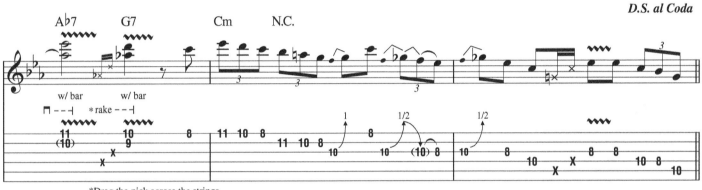

*Drag the pick across the strings indicated with a single motion.

⊕ **Coda**

care-free and wild, ___ but I got cat class and I got cat style. ___

Outro
N.C.
(Bass & drums)

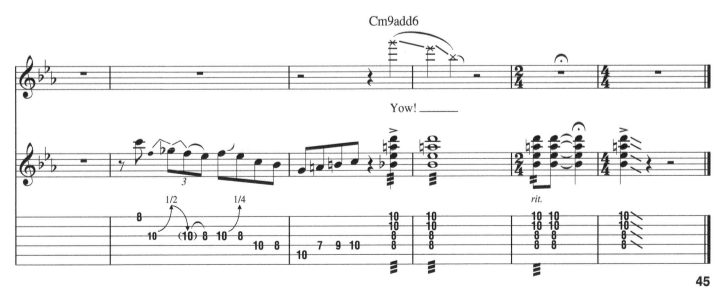

Yow! ___

That'll Be the Day

Words and Music by Jerry Allison, Norman Petty and Buddy Holly

*Symbols in parentheses reflect chord names respective to capoed guitar.
Symbols above reflect actual sounding chords. Capoed fret is "0" in tab.

all your hugs and kiss - es and your   mon - ey too. ___ Well, _ a,   you know you love me, ba - by.

P.M. ------------

D.S. al Coda 1
To Coda 2 ⊕

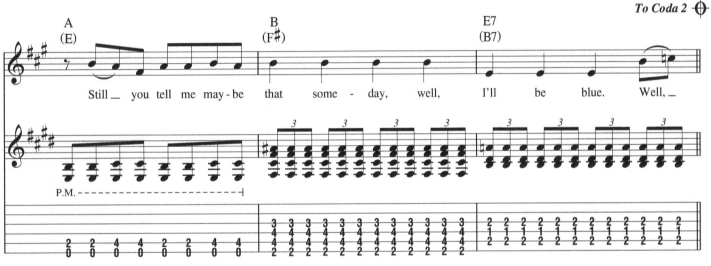

Still ___ you tell me may - be that   some - day,   well,   I'll   be   blue.   Well, ___

P.M. ------------

⊕ **Coda 1**

Guitar Solo

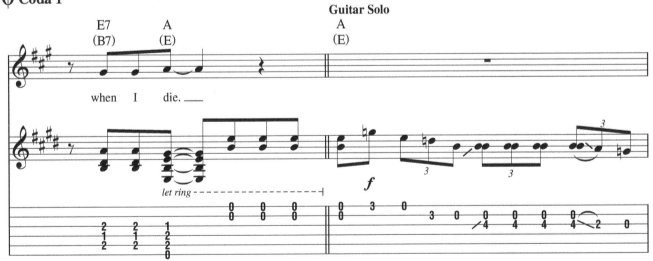

when   I   die. ___

let ring ------------

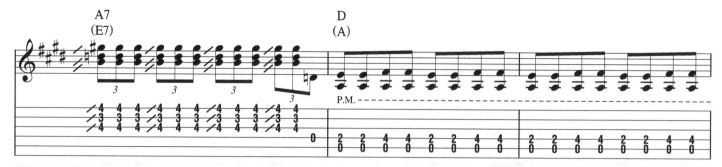

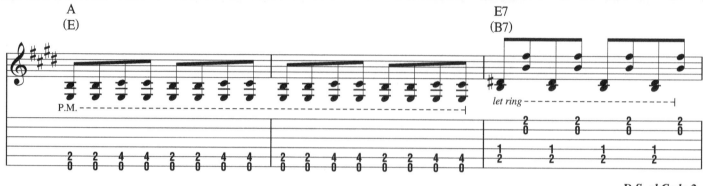

D.S. al Coda 2

Well,

Coda 2

Chorus

That-'ll be the day when you say good-bye. Yes,_____

that-'ll be the day when you make me cry.___ You say you're gon-na leave. You

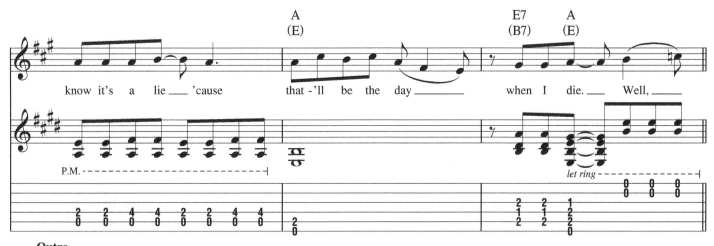

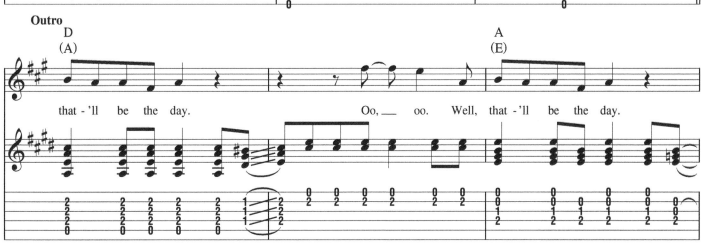

Outro

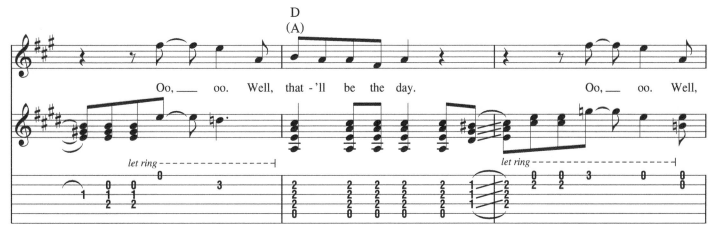

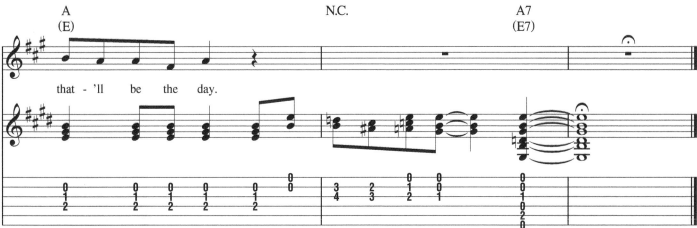

Additional Lyrics

2. Well, a, when Cupid shot his dart,
He shot it at your heart,
So if we ever part then I'll leave you.
You sit and hold me and you tell me boldly
That someday, well, I'll be blue.

Mystery Train

Words and Music by Sam C. Phillips and Herman Parker Jr.

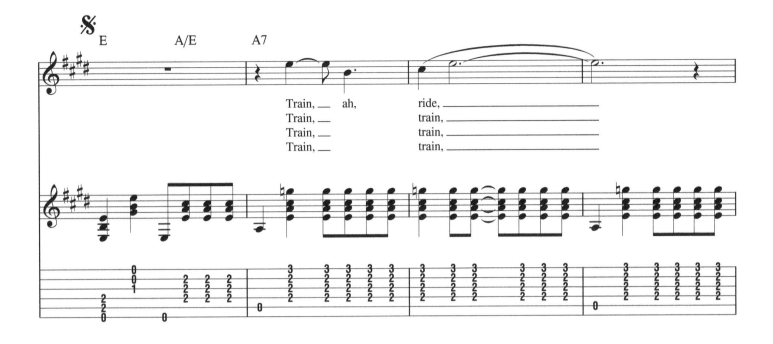

Train, __ ah, ride, _____
Train, __ train, _____
Train, __ train, _____
Train, __ train, _____

six - teen _____ coach - es long. _____
com - in' _____ 'round the bend. _____
com - in' _____ down the line. _____
com - in' __ 'round, 'round the bend. _____

Well, that long, __ black train _____
Well, it took __ my ba -
Well, it's bring - in' my ba -
Well, it took __ my ba -

A7

by,
by,
by

got my ba - by ___ and
but it nev - er will ___ a -
'cause she's mine, all, all
but it nev - er will ___ a -

To Coda ⊕

E   A/E   E   A/E   E   A/E   E   A/E

gone.
gain.
mine. ___ She's
gain,

No,
No,
mine, all, all
nev - er will a -

not a - gain.
mine.
gain.

1., 2.

3.

Guitar Solo

A7

A7

2. Train, _____
3. Train, _____

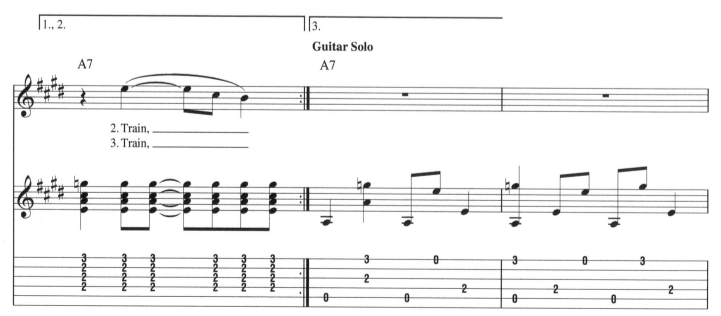

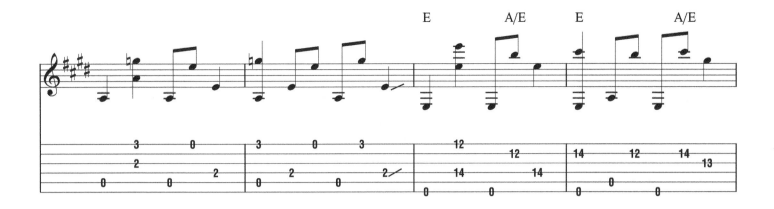

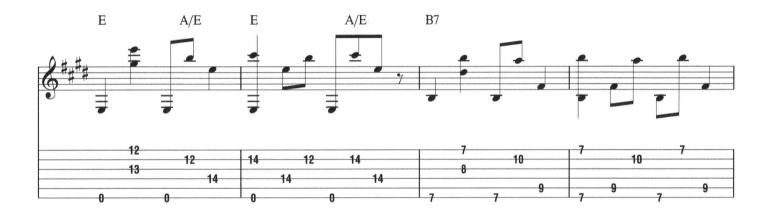

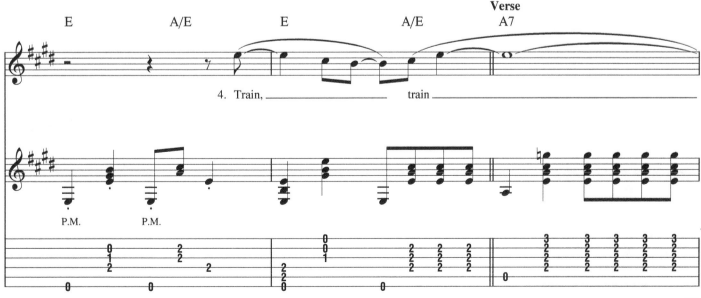

4. Train, _____ train _____

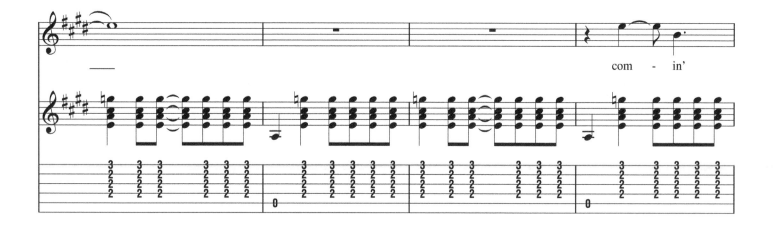

com - in'

D.S. al Coda

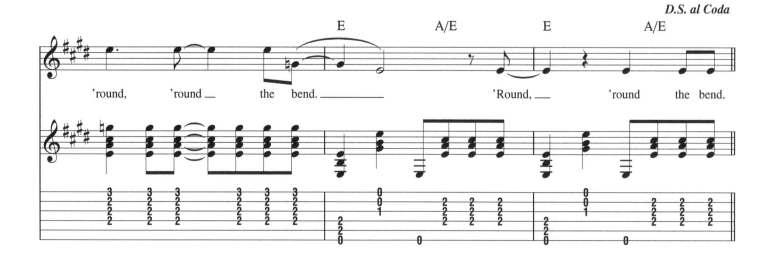

'round, 'round __ the bend. _____ 'Round, __ 'round the bend.

Coda

Outro

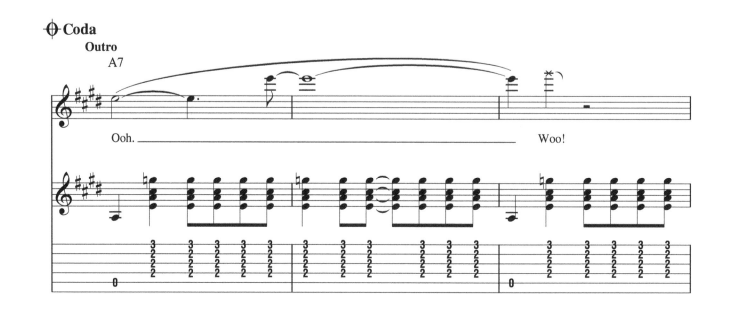

Ooh. _____ Woo!

Repeat and fade

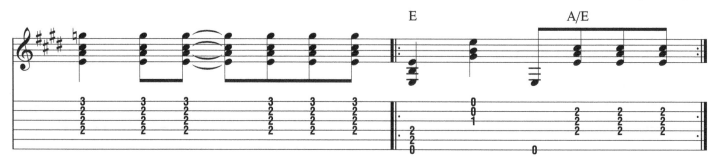

HAL•LEONARD GUITAR PLAY-ALONG

INCLUDES TAB

AUDIO ACCESS INCLUDED

This series will help you play your favorite songs quickly and easily. Just follow the tab and listen to the audio to hear how the guitar should sound, and then play along using the separate backing tracks.

Playback tools are provided for slowing down the tempo without changing pitch and looping challenging parts. The melody and lyrics are included in the book so that you can sing or simply follow along.

105. LATIN
00700939.....................$16.99

106. WEEZER
00700958.....................$14.99

107. CREAM
00701069.....................$16.99

108. THE WHO
00701053.....................$16.99

109. STEVE MILLER
00701054.....................$19.99

110. SLIDE GUITAR HITS
00701055.....................$16.99

111. JOHN MELLENCAMP
00701056.....................$14.99

112. QUEEN
00701052.....................$16.99

113. JIM CROCE
00701058.....................$17.99

114. BON JOVI
00701060.....................$16.99

115. JOHNNY CASH
00701070.....................$16.99

116. THE VENTURES
00701124.....................$17.99

117. BRAD PAISLEY
00701224.....................$16.99

118. ERIC JOHNSON
00701353.....................$16.99

119. AC/DC CLASSICS
00701356.....................$17.99

120. PROGRESSIVE ROCK
00701457.....................$14.99

121. U2
00701508.....................$16.99

122. CROSBY, STILLS & NASH
00701610.....................$16.99

123. LENNON & McCARTNEY ACOUSTIC
00701614.....................$16.99

124. SMOOTH JAZZ
00200664.....................$16.99

125. JEFF BECK
00701687.....................$17.99

126. BOB MARLEY
00701701.....................$17.99

127. 1970S ROCK
00701739.....................$16.99

128. 1960S ROCK
00701740.....................$14.99

129. MEGADETH
00701741.....................$17.99

130. IRON MAIDEN
00701742.....................$17.99

131. 1990S ROCK
00701743.....................$14.99

132. COUNTRY ROCK
00701757.....................$15.99

133. TAYLOR SWIFT
00701894.....................$16.99

134. AVENGED SEVENFOLD
00701906.....................$16.99

135. MINOR BLUES
00151350.....................$17.99

136. GUITAR THEMES
00701922.....................$14.99

137. IRISH TUNES
00701966.....................$15.99

138. BLUEGRASS CLASSICS
00701967.....................$17.99

139. GARY MOORE
00702370.....................$16.99

140. MORE STEVIE RAY VAUGHAN
00702396.....................$17.99

141. ACOUSTIC HITS
00702401.....................$16.99

142. GEORGE HARRISON
00237697.....................$17.99

143. SLASH
00702425.....................$19.99

144. DJANGO REINHARDT
00702531.....................$16.99

145. DEF LEPPARD
00702532.....................$19.99

146. ROBERT JOHNSON
00702533.....................$16.99

147. SIMON & GARFUNKEL
14041591.....................$16.99

148. BOB DYLAN
14041592.....................$16.99

149. AC/DC HITS
14041593.....................$17.99

150. ZAKK WYLDE
02501717.....................$19.99

151. J.S. BACH
02501730.....................$16.99

152. JOE BONAMASSA
02501751.....................$19.99

153. RED HOT CHILI PEPPERS
00702990.....................$19.99

155. ERIC CLAPTON – FROM THE ALBUM UNPLUGGED
00703085.....................$16.99

156. SLAYER
00703770.....................$19.99

157. FLEETWOOD MAC
00101382.....................$17.99

159. WES MONTGOMERY
00102593.....................$19.99

160. T-BONE WALKER
00102641.....................$17.99

161. THE EAGLES – ACOUSTIC
00102659.....................$17.99

162. THE EAGLES HITS
00102667.....................$17.99

163. PANTERA
00103036.....................$17.99

164. VAN HALEN 1986-1995
00110270.....................$17.99

165. GREEN DAY
00210343.....................$17.99

166. MODERN BLUES
00700764.....................$16.99

167. DREAM THEATER
00111938.....................$24.99

168. KISS
00113421.....................$17.99

169. TAYLOR SWIFT
00115982.....................$16.99

170. THREE DAYS GRACE
00117337.....................$16.99

171. JAMES BROWN
00117420.....................$16.99

172. THE DOOBIE BROTHERS
00116970.....................$16.99

173. TRANS-SIBERIAN ORCHESTRA
00119907.....................$19.99

174. SCORPIONS
00122119.....................$16.99

175. MICHAEL SCHENKER
00122127.....................$17.99

176. BLUES BREAKERS WITH JOHN MAYALL & ERIC CLAPTON
00122132.....................$19.99

177. ALBERT KING
00123271.....................$16.99

178. JASON MRAZ
00124165.....................$17.99

179. RAMONES
00127073.....................$16.99

180. BRUNO MARS
00129706.....................$16.99

181. JACK JOHNSON
00129854.....................$16.99

182. SOUNDGARDEN
00138161.....................$17.99

183. BUDDY GUY
00138240.....................$17.99

184. KENNY WAYNE SHEPHERD
00138258.....................$17.99

185. JOE SATRIANI
00139457.....................$17.99

186. GRATEFUL DEAD
00139459.....................$17.99

187. JOHN DENVER
00140839.....................$17.99

188. MÖTLEY CRUE
00141145.....................$17.99

189. JOHN MAYER
00144350.....................$17.99

190. DEEP PURPLE
00146152.....................$17.99

191. PINK FLOYD CLASSICS
00146164.....................$17.99

192. JUDAS PRIEST
00151352.....................$17.99

193. STEVE VAI
00156028.....................$19.99

194. PEARL JAM
00157925.....................$17.99

195. METALLICA: 1983-1988
00234291.....................$19.99

196. METALLICA: 1991-2016
00234292.....................$19.99

HAL•LEONARD®

For complete songlists, visit
Hal Leonard online at
www.halleonard.com

Prices, contents, and availability subject to
change without notice.

1120
9/12; 397